Antonio Elster

AF286464

How your small ideas & inventions make big money

German Patent Protection for 40 Euro

GERMAN TITLE:
Deutscher Patentschutz für 40 Euro
Wie Ihre kleinen Ideen & Erfindungen großes Geld verdienen

IO

IMPRESSUM ENGLISH

Printed figures, prices, addresses, procedures and all other informations and representations can change fast, mistakes can happen and the individual conditions of the readers are generally different: Thus, all informations contained herein serve merely the orientation. They represent no recommendation or instruction for concrete approaches. They do not claim completeness, and they are to be understood only as non-binding information. In every single case the reader is asked to investigate further in detail. The possible use of described data and procedures is done at own risk. No liability whatsoever accepted.

The copyright as well as all other rights in this title are left exclusively to the author. A liability of the author or the publishing company for personal, material, property and all the other damages is excluded. Print and other mistakes are reserved.

No part of this publication may be reproduced, stored in or introduced into a retrieval system, or transmitted, in any form or by any means (electronic, mechanical, photocopying, recording, or otherwise) without the prior written permission of the author. The scanning, uploading, and distribution of this book or parts of it via the Internet or any other means without the prior written permission of the author is illegal and punishable by law.

Reprint and any other kind of duplication, as well as every handing-over of illegal reprints of this book, be it the entire text or parts of it, is not permitted: Every single case of duplication, spreading, translation, storage – including every individual transfer onto electronic data carriers like DVD, CD, flash memory, hard disks, floppy disks, magnetic tape etc. – *is not permitted without written approval of the author and is punishable and is pursued by law.* This copyright applies also to the using and/or showing of the entire text or part of it in electronic media like in Internet-discussion forums and to the publication by so-called "Search-Inside" functions.

Antonio Elster: How your small ideas and inventions make big money: German Patent Protection For 40 Euros

Copyright © 2010 Antonio Elster. All rights reserved. 2. english Edition. Title, text and cover creation by Antonio Elster. Production and publishing company BOD GmbH, Norderstedt, Germany. ISBN 978-3-8334-9494-9. Printed in Germany in 2010

IMPRESSUM DEUTSCH

Gedruckte Zahlen-, Preis-, Adreß-, Verfahrens- und alle sonstigen Angaben und Darstellungen können sich schnell ändern, Fehler können geschehen und die individuellen Ausgangs-voraussetzungen der Leser sind im Allgemeinen sehr unterschiedlich: Daher dienen grundsätzlich alle Angaben in diesem Buch lediglich der Orientierung. Sie stellen keine Empfehlung oder Anleitung für konkrete Vorgehensweisen dar. Sie erheben keinen Anspruch auf Vollständigkeit, und sie sind ausschließlich als unverbindliche Information zu verstehen. In jedem Einzelfall ist der Leser gebeten, sich ausführlich weitergehend zu informieren. Die eventuelle Verwendung von beschriebenen Daten und Verfahren erfolgt ausschließlich auf eigenes Risiko. Es wird keinerlei Haftung übernommen.

Das Urheberrecht sowie sämtliche anderen Rechte an diesem Buchtitel sind ausschließlich dem Autor vorbehalten. Eine Haftung des Autors oder des Verlages für Personen-, Sach-, Vermögens-und alle anderen Schäden ist ausgeschlossen. Druck- und andere Fehler vorbehalten.

Nachdruck und jede andere Art der Vervielfältigung, sowie jede vervielfältigte Zuverfügungstellung dieses Buches, oder einzelner Teile daraus, ist ausdrücklich *nicht gestattet:* Jeder Einzelfall von Vervielfältigung, Verbreitung, Übersetzung, Speicherung – einschließlich jeder individuellen Übertragung auf elektronische Datenträger wie DVD, CD, Speicherkarte, flüchtige und nicht-flüchtige Speicherbausteine, Computerfestplatte, Diskette, Magnetband usw. – *ist ohne schriftliche Genehmigung des Autors unzulässig und strafbar, und wird strafrechtlich verfolgt.* Audrücklich gilt dieses Verbot auch für die Zuverfügungstellung des Buchtitels in elektronischen Medien – etwa die vollständige oder auszugsweise Textverwendung in Internet-Diskussionsforen, und die Veröffentlichung mittels sogenannter "Search-Inside"-Funktionen.

Antonio Elster: How your small ideas & inventions make big money: German Patent Protection For 40 Euros

Copyright © 2010 Antonio Elster. 2. englische Auflage. Titelbild/Einbandgestaltung Antonio Elster. Alle Rechte vorbehalten. Herstellung und Verlag BOD GmbH, Norderstedt, Deutschland. ISBN 978-3-8334-9494-9. Printed in Germany 2010

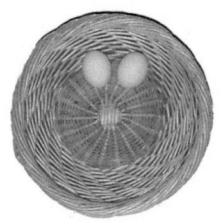

Protecting Good Ideas

Ever since the time that humans have been conscious about their own existence and thus the inconvenience of everyday life, they have been searching and developing to make a better life. This efforts resulted in new discoveries, over and over again. These discoveries then led to products which made, and make, life either more comfortable, cheaper, faster or all of these.

However, before a new product arrives in reality, people must develop new ideas first. New ideas of which an improvement can initially only be assumed. In fact, this is the case with many individuals: Who hadn't thoughts like: "...one would have to.." ? Unrestrained curiosity and an obvious innate urge to live a more comfortable life seem to positively direct into new ideas: In many cases successful innovations develop from small inconveniences or emergencies in daily life.

If this almost difficult-to-understand loads of human innovation power would not exist - our world would be an entirely different one: Aside from a dangerous and dull cave life with an average life duration of only 25 years, art and culture would and could not exist: Well working technologies are necessary even for the wonderful paintings by Michelangelo or for the productive cultivation of wheat. In order to discover and develop these technologies, someone must have had deep thoughts somewhere in time. In this sense,

3

the thinkers and inventors of our world – in general: all individuals deeply interested in mechanics, electricity, chemistry and other scientific fields – are the only friends of humankind. They are the only real improvers of the world who deserve this title.

But which intelligent and attentive restless minds way back in time have invented the artful form of paint-brush binding, the longer-lasting color pigment or the sawing machine? And, were the long days and months and costs necessary worthwhile for these genius heads? We all unfortunately know: Except for a few, those persons who brought mankind forward step by step are mostly unknown.

Only in the most favorable cases the prospect for fame and wealth goes along with a new idea. Just think about Albert Einstein. The publication of his new physical theory[1] - which hardly anyone understood (. . . and understands, one might add) and which til today affects the life of almost all of us – made him quickly a world-famous man.

For other examples one does not even need to look that high. In the "lowlands" of the tangible everyday products, names like Edison or Diesel are familiar to everyone. These meticulous inventors discovered still big, fundamental, up to then unknown innovations, which affected entire economic sectors. It was for this reason that they favored the establishment of own enterprises and thus - not always, but often - fame and financial success were ensured.

However, most new ideas were in former times, are today and will be in the future the "small" improvements: This ideas won't touch the basics of physics. They won't employ unknown Laws of Nature. And they won't deliver opportunities for the development of new industries. That is, because fundamental discoveries become ever more difficult

---

[1] ...in combination with proofs of correctness

4

for individuals because the necessary laboratory equipment becomes increasingly complex and thereby expensive.

But that doesn't really matter. Even apparently small, at first sight rather inconspicuous ideas can possess an immense potential: They can be manufactered more easily. Also, the entire process of projecting is easier to handle. Further, it is simple and cheap to manufacture a functioning prototype. Then, it is easy to monitor the production. And last but not least, small and cheap products usually target the mass-market, which often promises high quantities and therefore a high turn-over. Potential licensees are attracted by these advantages, which again increases the possibility of successful marketing. From the viwepoint of the individual inventor it can be much more rewarding to concentrate on the research and development of small improvements for daily use rather than hunting large world-changing ideas.

After a functioning idea has been developed, the issue of protecting it quickly emerges. In order to offer each owner of a thinking machine protection of the results of his/her machine – and by that beeing able to enjoy the merits of his/her intellectual property instead of leaving it collecting dust – many countries worldwide have established a patent authority, the so-called Patent Office[2].

A Patent Office distributes and administrates rights on new ideas, products and techniques through the patenting procedure. It further informs the public about these rights and it possesses decision power, if controversies arise. In Germany, the patent authority is called *Deutsches Patent- und Marken-amt (German Patent and Trade Mark Office)*. It is a sub-ordinate agency of the Federal Ministry of Law, and has it´s headquarter office in Munich, the capital city of Bavaria:

---

[2] There are quite a number of further, partially very selfish reasons, why a state offers patenting.

5

Deutsches Patent- und Markenamt
(German Patent- and Trade Mark Office)
Zweibrückenstraße 12
80331 München (Germany)
Telephone (089) 2195 – 0
Telefax (089) 2195 - 2221
Internet: www.dpma.de

Postal Address
Deutsches Patent- und Markenamt
80297 München, Germany

So what is "patenting", anyway ? Patenting in fact is no more than a registration of a new technical idea, connected to an individual name on a particular date. By that, a relatively safe protection is created: Unauthorized individuals or companies must not use protected third party intellectual property free of charge, for example by manufacturing and selling. As such, a patent protects against cheap copying and imitation.

If existing property rights (that is very important: they must be brought into existence first.) are infringed, then the cause of action is given: Payment of damages can be claimed. While this sounds simple – reality often shows otherwise. Aside from the difficulty of accurate descriptions, in patenting, time is a crucial factor: It is very important who was first in a registration process. The national systems and the adherent mentalities differ in part substantially. Just look at the United States and Germany (Europe): In the U.S., anybody can become a registered patentee, if he or she is able to prove that he/she *had* the very idea first. Not so in Germany: Here, anybody can become an official patentee, who *registered* the particular idea first! Thus, the U.S. system seems to be more just and fair, but sometimes it might call for proofs difficult to deliver. In

Germany on the contrary, anybody can "copy" a good idea, which he, say, saw in the friend´s garage, and register it in his or her own name. By that, he/she actually becomes the legal patentee – if the true inventor is not ahead of him or her! If you, Dear Reader, already have a good idea worth protecting in your mind, then the first conclusion to be drawn from this is:

1. Let nobody share in it, **and**

2. register it immediately in order to secure the earliest possible date of registration.

In addition, it is worthwhile to note that not few people develop into downright perfectionists during their idea elaboration: If at all, many inventors think about protection only after their idea almost reached the stage of series production. But then it can be already too late. It is advisable to submit a patent application as early as possible – for example, immediately after finishing a functioning prototype. That is because your very first receipt of your application form the Patent Office will bear the already recorded the entry date. That calendar date will be one of the most important data concerning your later patent: It will be the hub for the entire registration and for all patent ambiguity and disputes, which might or might not arise in the future.

AN IMPORTANT NOTE

Even if your idea seems small or insignificant to you: We generally recommend registering good ideas as Utility Patents, and as soon as possible that is. The process requires little time and money only. The opportunities on the other hand can be huge. Just think about it:

Should really somebody else make money on your good idea ? Indeed, that wouldn´t be. . .what the inventor had in mind, would it ?

... and making money with them

There are several possibilities to exploit existing patent rights. Production, marketing and selling in the own name is just one of those. The sale of production and/or distribution rights, commonly called the licensing, is another. The latter one is also the most frequently used option.

Choosing the first option, the inventor needs very good organizational skills. Usually, he also needs quite a lot of money to get the production and/or the selling going from zero. How much easier is the second option, which should be the first for most people ! There, one needs "simply" to find a promising licensee and to negotiate and close successfully a rewarding license agreement. In this license agreement it will be agreed upon in writing that

- the owner of a patent as licensor
- gives permission to
- a certain contracting party as licensee
- to completely or partially use
- this patent right
- against the payment of one or more fees.

The license thus specifies, to what extent and under what conditions a licensee may (or must) use the protected idea. Examples of what can be specified are

- the duration of the contract
- the kind of license (production license or distribution license, or both)
- the authorized market regions (Federal State, Germany, Europe, worldwide)

- the sublicence provision (is a subsale permitted, or is it not ?)
- the minimum quantities to be produced
- the terms and time frame of payments

Restrictions may be imposed upon the licensee in almost any aspect, however, these restrictions may concern the patent right only. Otherwise the Antitrust Law would be infringed upon.

Quickly then, the question arises whether a simple or an exclusive license should be sold. An exclusive license transfers all rights on the invention to the licensee. It can be limited, however, according to its kind - for example, as exclusive production license only, or as exclusive distribution license only. In these cases the licensee possesses the exclusive warrant on the patent right: If no appropriate clause is contained in the license agreement, then even the inventor loses his/her rights on the product for the duration of the contract!

With the *simple license* however, the licenser keeps rights over his/her product. It is thus possible to sell several licenses to different licensees. The question for the inventor whether a simple or an exclusive license would be the better choice - emerges only if actually there is a choice: This, however, is often not the case. Most buyers, the licensees, have exact conceptions about what they want and what they do not want: It is often that simple.

Important again is the question about the royalty payments. Any number of possible and "impossible" payment schemes can be used. The amount of payments depends primarily on the product potential and on the kind of contract, simple or exclusive. And, of course, the amounts to be paid depend on the negotiating skills of both parties. Usually, an exclusive license is more expensive than a simple license. As soon as one starts detailed thinking about a license agreement one will discover that

- many topics have to be arranged in detail and
- often interesting financial dimensions are concerned and
- both contracting parties are often in the habit of wrong memory.

Thus, license agreements should always be put in writing. Always. Also it is hardly ever recommendable to use a model contract or to simply copy an existing license agreement: Individual conditions are very rarely to be compared with others.

The private licenser should also pay attention not to be misled by the often experienced licensees like directors or company attorneys. And yes, it is as important the other way around: To keep both feet firmly on ground and avoid expecting heaven by unreasonable estimations.

Before a license agreement can even be negotiated, a licensee interested in your patent has to be found. Probably quite soon you will find out, that this is anything but a simple task: Sure, you could ask around among acquaintances, visit fairs and the like. However, the most effective procedure however is to address a number of appropriate companies directly. Large data bases, as for instance *Who supplies what* (German: Wer liefert was?) and the Internet are good sources, which within seconds deliver potentially interested companies including their phone numbers and addresses. Calling them, finding the right person to talk to and get interest in the own idea is the difficult part. If you get to the point, where you are permitted to a presentation of your functioning product prototype, then you are right on track.

This, by the way, is an all important point: Experience shows again and again that a functioning prototype, which can be looked at and tried is a, if not t h e base condition for success. The inventor *must* be able to show and demonstrate his or her product. It does not have to look perfect, it may even work just in an improvised way – but it must function! However professional well chosen words and nice business suits may seem – do yourself a very big favor by showing a real and working prototype. Period.

After a potential licensee has been found, he often possesses deeper insights in the Law on Contracts and the contract design than the individual inventor does. Many risks lurk here, but then, also many opportunities. For the unexperienced, even for the semi-experienced inventor, it is quite often advisable from this point of time on to get advice from a lawyer. If you plan to do so please remember: This is about the most favorable *contract terms to your advantage.* Therefore, it might not be necessary to talk to a patent lawyer. Perhaps, an experienced contract lawyer might even be the better choice.

The German Utility Patent

The German Utility Model Application (German: Das Gebrauchsmuster), in short the Utility Patent, is frequently referred to as the "small brother" of the regular patent. That is not completely unjustified: Because the Utility Patent is indeed an adequate Patent Protection Right, which for starters just means a record of a newly invented product or technical procedure. High concordances exist between both Patent Rights, and so are some differences. The most important advantages of the Utility Patent in comparison to the "normal" Patent are due to the

1. **substantially lower costs,**

2. **quick processing, and**

3. **simplicity of the registration procedure.**

Are there any disadvantages at all ? Yes, there are: An Utility Patent can be applied only to real technical "things", it can't be used for procedures or other theoretical matters. Also, the maximum duration of protection by the Utility Patent is only half of that of a regular patent (10 vs. 20 years). And, it is governed by national law, which means that Utility Patents protect in Germany only. But all of this does not have to be unfavorable, because there are very substantial advantages: A patent application usually takes years until the patent itself is

13

finally granted. Often accompanied by immense financial requirements, which are hard to cope with by the average individual citizen. The Utility Patent in contrast is registered in a few weeks time, and the costs involved are really small.

One particular characteristic is the *period preclusive of prejudice to novelty* of six months: For up to six months after publication of the idea, for example during a fair, the inventor can still register it as Utility Patent. In contrast with the regular patent: A patent can only be registered if the invention was not publicly known at the time of the registration; as the case may be, the presentation of the product on the fair would have prevented the entire patenting! Also in the criterion of the *inventive step* the Utility Patent shows its advantages. While with the patent application the inventive achievement is closely examined and evaluated, the Utility Patent gives more freeways. Smaller ideas are therewith appreciated.

In real life, the disadvantages of the Utility Patent compared to the "normal" patent are often far smaller for private applicants than for large enterprises – therefore the Utility Patent is particularly well fitting for smaller inventions by people like you and me. Since many ideas can be protected both ways, the denotation *Small Brother* is a little too modest and thus a little misdirecting.

1. Possible registration applicants:
Who can protect his idea?

a) Each person with legal residence in Germany can register a utility patent. This can be done completely on own. Representation by an attorney or a patent lawyer is possible at any time, even later in the process – but remains voluntarily.

b) <u>Persons who do not have a legal residence and no permanent establishment in Germany</u>, for example of their company, can likewise apply for a Utility Patent. However, they must have themselve represented by a (free to choose) lawyer or attorney headquarted in Germany for the validity period of the patent right (up to 10 years). Representation by the lawyer has to start from the first application form on.

2. My idea or yours ?

By the above mentioned German invention registration principle it became clear who can register a new idea or product: Whoever registers first will get the patent rights for this idea. This applies to all individuals.

Employees though represent a special case: In Germany they may have to register own inventions through the so-called employee invention patent. This applies, whenever the idea in question is connected with their field of work at the employers company. This complication does not develop out of the utility patent, but applies to each kind of patent registration, thus also to the regular patent: An employed molding cutter for example may not be allowed to register his newly developed design of a special molding cut in his own name, but must register it in the name of his employer, or through registration by his employer. The law differentiates between *business operation inventions* and *free inventions* of employees. A business operation invention exists,

- if the invention originated while the employment contract was valid,

- and if it is based either on the incumbent activity of the employee, or on the experience and activity of the employee in the company.

In all of these cases the employee must inform the employer about the invention. The employer must thereupon either present it for patenting, or release the invention for the benefit of the employee. If the employer claims the invention, then most rights on it are transferred to the employer. However, an appropriate remuneration must be paid to the inventor. Often it is not entirely clear what exactly "appropriate" means: The remuneration sum is a function of the economic usefulness, as well as of the portion of the enterprise in the originating of the business operation invention.

A *free invention* on teh other hand does not have to be submitted to the employer. However, the employee must inform the employer sufficiently about the invention. The meaning of "sufficiently" here is: The employer must receive at least that much information, that he will be able to evaluate whether it actually concerns a free invention. If within a three months period no appeal is made, then the invention is free: It cannot be claimed anymore as a business operation invention.

3. What kind of ideas and products can be protected ?

Common to the two patent rights "Utility Patent" and "normal" Patent are the basic conditions for their assignation: Both must be about ideas acceptable for registration. "Acceptable for registration" by the standard of the German Patent Office means: The new ideas or products have to be

1. new technical inventions,
2. based on a real inventive step, and

16

3. commercially applicable.

1. An **innovation** in the meaning used exists, if the idea or the product does not already belong to a presently or previously existing technology or knowledge. "Available technology" refers to all knowledge which was publicly accessible up to the date of registration.

2. An **inventive step** means to go beyond the present available technology and the pure technical ability. The new product or idea must solve a problem, which was not solved up to then. It may not be obvious. However, the requirements for inventive steps in regard to a Utility Patent are lower than for the regular patent: Even smaller ideas have a good chance.

3. **Commercial applicability** means that the product or idea has to be able to be sensibly manufactured and/or used in commercial or agricultural fields.

Now, one question arises quickly: Who actually judges whether my idea fulfills these basic conditions? In the case of the Utility Patent Registration the answer is very simple: Nobody. That is because Utility Patents are examined exclusively for form, formulation and completeness at application. Actual contents are of no interest at all at that time! This is a strong characteristic of the Utility Patent: In order to make the filing process more economical and quick, no patent (if you will: no technical) examination takes place initially. The registration will be conducted only formally: Your idea, your name and the date of filing will be registered in a particular form, and that is it. At this point of time, no examination of technical content will take place. Immediatelly after the utility patent document is granted and sent out to you or to your representative by mail.

The entire procedure remains purposefully under the right of revoking by the Patent Office. A revoking happens for instance, if, at any time in the future, an earlier registration by somebody else than yours comes to light. Or, if your registration is invalid for scientific reasons, say, you claimed to discovered a perpetuum mobile. Also, a declaration of invalidity will be issued after it turned out that one or more registration conditions are not fulfilled.

An official search, which brings these things to light, more about it later on, is available for a fee and can be requested by anyone at any time. For example, by the inventor himself or by competing companies. Since the Search fee according to the applicable rates (2007) is substantially higher than the registration fee (250 vs. 40 Euro), only one conclusion remains: Register first, then see what happens.

Aside from technical devices and apparatuses, chemical materials, food, medicaments and micro organisms can also be protected by the Utility Patent. Protecting technical objects of all kinds is thus no problem, like a new design of a screw or a new door opener. The rule of thumb here is: If the product is touchable (...and completely, or partly, new), then it can be protected as a utility patent.

This flexible system, almost unexpectedly pragmatic for Germany, is the main reason for the small filing costs and for the short time of processing. Each inventor should use this to his advantage: Rather register too many ideas than too few. And what if your Utility Patent will be declared void sometime in the future ? Well, so what? There are people spending 40 Euros for Lotto each week. . .

Not allowed or *not* suitable for the protection by a Utility Patent are (excerpt):

- Procedures, for example production or manufacturing processes, measuring procedures

- Handling procedures

- Scientific theories and mathematical methods

- Constructions against the Laws of Nature, thus all kinds of Perpetuum Mobile

- Aesthetic forms of creations

- Species of plants or animals

- Rules, for example for games or record keeping systems

- Software

- "Forgotten" knowledge. So-called peoples' knowledge cannot be protected, because it existed publicly before the registration and therefore does not fulfill the registration criteria.

One further restriction exists: Inventions, which publication or utilization would offend Law and Order or the good morals can likewise not be protected. For example, one could imagine a reliably functioning radar-flash protection for car drivers, making license numbers on flash-photos illegible. This function could theoretically fulfill the criterion "..the publication or utilization offends Law and Order" and the registration could therefore be refused. But: No inventor has to tie himself/herself down to a certain use or name of his or her new idea. Neither by the selected product designation nor by the desciption of his idea in his/her application. So, the same equipment could be a "protection against identification of military license numbers in the public commuter traffic" as well and thereby could be registered without limitation.

4. The Search: Does it exist already ?

As already addressed above, at the beginning of a patent application it is not neccesarily clear whether the new idea is really new. To find out, the inventor himself can investigate the data bases of the Patent Office. Or he/she can – either at the time of registration or at any time after - assign the Patent Office to conduct an official search. Still, there is no obligation for a official search. However, a search can also be requested at any time by arbitrary third persons, for example by a potential licensee or by a competitor.

The search fee amounts to 250 Euro and is to be paid by the person requesting the search. After finishing the search, both the applicant and the inventor will receive a report. This report will list all patents by number and description, which *m i g h t* be applicable for the evaluation of the patentability of the own Utility Patent.

20

A conclusive decision won't be made by the search result rather than determined, which third party patents have to be considered. Since these questions often concern accurately determining which formulations could and should protect exactly what sometimes, single words play a crucial role in the Description and in the Claims. Should thereupon the Patent Office declare a cancellation request as valid, then from that date on only that Utility Patent or regular patent is recognized, which was registered first. Others will be deleted. If, on the other hand, the own Utility Patent withstands this examination, then it possesses almost the same value as any other registered and valid patent. "Almost", because in some cases the limited protection period (10 years compared to 20 years) can financially work out unfavorably. But – under certain conditions Utility Patents can still be converted into a patent at a later time. It would then receive the prolonged protection period of 20 years.

5. Costs and protection period

A huge advantage of the Utility Patent lies in its small costs. The entire application fee actually amounts to 40 Euros only. Fullfilled conditions regarding originality, form etc. assumed, the Utility Patent then is good for three years for this tiny amount. The 3-year period begins on the first submit date as recorded by the Patent Office. After that three years, the patent right can, but does not have to, be extended three times, up to altogether 10 years of duration. The extension fees due as of 2010 follow this pattern:

4. – 6. year: 210 Euro

7. – 8. year: 350 Euro

9. – 10. year: 530 Euro

This fees are due at expiration date of the third, sixth and eight year, on the last day of the registration month. There is a two-month time allowance for payment. If the fees nevertheless won`t be deposited within this period, a small fine of 50 Euro becomes due. If the fees are still not paid after six months beyond the expiration date, then the Utility Patent expires without further notice. **Only the applicant and/or the Utility Patent owner is responsible for the timely payment of all fees.**
Payments can be made both in cash in the Patent Office in Munich or its subsidieries, or through usual bank wire. In case of bank wires, the day of receipt at the Patent Office is the legal date of payment. Important with bank transfers: Always indicate the file reference and the intended purpose of the payment (..which is a standardized number: the fee code, see further down).

6. How do I register ?

If the decision to register a Utility Patent has been made, then the procedure is as mentioned below, given as a summary for better overview. Detailed explanations will follow in the next chapter. Applicants with no German residence must assign a lawyer (who has not necessarily to be a patent lawyer) to represent them. Also, in order to receive an as early as possible patenting date, you will be allowed to submit your application initially in English (or any other) language in order to secure an early as possible registration date. However, soon after you will receive a request to submit a certified translation into German language. The steps from Zero to patent owner read as follows:

1. Obtain, fill out and sign the official Application Form (one A4 sheet with only few data).

2. Write down the so-called *Description* of your idea (no particular form).

3. Write down the so-called *Claims* for your idea (no particular form).

4. Make *Drawings* (no particular form). Drawings are not a mandatory part of the application.

5. Number all sheets consecutively and send them in duplicated to the Patent Office.

6. Wait until the acknowledgement of receipt by the Patent Office arrives by mail. This takes only a few days. The receipt will show a punched and thereby confirmed starting date as well as the file reference number.

7. Pay the application fee of 40 Euro, indicating the file reference number. If the fee is not paid within three months, your application is considered revoked without further notice.

8. Wait for further mail and answer if necessary. The Patent Office quite often notifies about reformulating desires or criticizes the form of the submission.

9. The Utility Patent certificate is sent to you by mail.

7. How long does the entire application take ?

Usually the time needed is pleasingly short. If no unusual difficulties arise, within 2 to 4 months the Utility Patent certificate is sent to you or to your representative by mail.

8. Do I need a lawyer ?

Each legal resident in Germany may register his/her Utility Patent without assistance from a lawyer. Also, even in mid-process, the applicant is free to hand over the entire case or parts of it to a lawyer of choice. Advice from a lawyer is probably appropriate during the formulation of the Claims for most people. This is because the protective effect and thus the later value of the patent rights are determined by it. In addition and according to experience, few people find it fun and easy to formulate the unfamiliar "patent language".
Patent lawyers are suited for this task because of their technical training in combination with their legal training. On the Internet for instance, you will find many lawyers at *www. Patentanwaltsuche.de* (English: patent lawyer search). If you do not live in Germany, and neither have a registered office here (company, agency etc.), you *must* be represented by a lawyer at any time.

9. Helpful documents

Besides many others, the following documents are available to inventors free of charge on the Internet server of the German Patent Office in Munich. The Numbers designate the internal form name of the Patent Office.

- Informations for Utility Model applicants: G6181.1 (English); G6181 (German)
- Information about expenses: A9510
- Application form for a Utility Patent (German: Antrag auf Eintragung eines Gebrauchsmusters): G6003
- Ordinance implementing the Utility Model Law: G6180.1 (English); G6180 (German)

BUNDESREPUBLIK DEUTSCHLAND

URKUNDE

über die Eintragung des

Gebrauchsmusters

Nr. 3 12 700.5

IPC: 67C 11/06

Bezeichnung:
Überlaufschutz für Flüssigkeitstrichter

Gebrauchsmusterinhaber:
Faber,Teri, 61250 Usingen, DE

Tag der Anmeldung: 18.08.2005

Tag der Eintragung: 13.11.2005

Der Präsident des Deutschen Patent- und Markenamts

Dr. Schade

How it looks: The official Patent Document

26

Your Registration

Like always when interacting with authorities, the German Patent- and Trademark Office provides and requires all kinds of forms, requests, instruction cards and form requirements. Any complete application for a Utility Patent consists of at least 3 documents, which are mandatory in any case. These three papers are:

1. The **Application Form,** consisting of a single A4 sheet (the European letter format). It contains only a few fields to be filled-in, which even unexperienced people probably will find easy to do.

2. The technical **Description** of the invention or idea (no form). The Description should explain the new idea to technically educated people in a way that the reader is able to actual manufacture the product.

3. The **Claims** of the invention or idea (no form). The Claims describe as accurately as possible, which particular characteristics of the new product the applicant wishes to have protected in his or her name.

These 3 documents are the minimum requirement. Depending on personal circumstances, additional forms or authority letters

27

have to be added, for instance a signed Power of Attorney form.

All documents and sheets of an application are to be submitted in double. The language used is typically German. However, an application can also be submitted in a different language, for example to quickly secure the date of entry. In this case authenticated translations to German language must be supplied within three months. If the translations are not supplied within this period, the entire application will be considered revoked.

Great attention, if not solely attention, is paid by the Patent Office to the outer appearance and to the formulations of your application. Below, you will find an excerpt from the general form requirements. The complete set of requirements can be taken either from instruction leaflets, which are available in English too or directly from the Patent Offices Webserver. To many people the bureaucrazy seems a little overdone. But one could keep in mind that the Patent Office receives many thousands of most different ideas each single year. All of these ideas have to be recorded, archived, and most important – must be able to retrace them quickly, even after years. And yes, sometimes patent rights worth hundreds of thousands of Euros are derived from these procedures. If you think about all this, the formal requirements do no longer appear completely from outer space.

Excerpt from the form requirements

- Paper sheet size exclusively the A4 format.
- With exception of Drawings, all sheets must be presented in portrait orientation.
- All sheets must be written on one side only.
- The line spacing must be 1.5

- Minimum margins are: At the top and on the left 2.5 centimeters, at the right and at the bottom 2.0 centimeters.
- No handwriting: Typewriter or computer printer are the only ones permitted.
- Only white and clean printer paper is to be used
- Paper sheets must be clean, no tears and edges, sharp bends or erasures.

1. The official Application Form

An das
Deutsche Patent- und Markenamt
80297 München

DEUTSCHES PATENT- UND MARKENAMT

(1) Sendungen des Deutschen Patent- und Markenamts sind zu richten an:

Anschrift
Straße,
Haus-Nr.
und ggf.
Postfach
angeben

☐ **Antrag auf Eintragung eines Gebrauchsmusters**

☐ **Eintritt in die nationale Phase Aktenzeichen PCT/ . . . / . . . .**

☐ TELEFAX vorab am

2

Aktenzeichen *(wird vom Deutschen Patent- und Markenamt vergeben)*

(2) Zeichen des Anmelders/Vertreters (max. 20 Stellen) | Telefon des Anmelders/Vertreters | Datum

(3) Der Empfänger in Feld (1) ist der | ggf. Nr. der Allgemeinen Vollmacht
☐ Anmelder ☐ Zustellungsbevollmächtigte ☐ Vertreter

(4) **Anmelder** **Vertreter**

nur auszu-
füllen, wenn
abwei-
chend
von
Feld
(1)

soweit (5) Anmeldercode-Nr. | Vertretercode-Nr. | Zustelladresscode-Nr.
bekannt

(6) **Bezeichnung der Erfindung**

unverbindl. IPC-Vorschlag d. Anmelders

(7) **Sonstige Anträge**

s. Kosten-
hinweise
auf der
Rückseite

☐ **Aussetzung der Eintragung und Bekanntmachung für** _____ Monate *(Max. 15 Monate ab Anmelde- bzw. Prioritätstag)*

☐ **Recherchenantrag** - Ermittlung der öffentlichen Druckschriften (§ 7 Gebrauchsmustergesetz)

(8) **Erklärungen**

Aktenzeichen | Anmeldetag

☐ **Teilung/Ausscheidung aus der Gebrauchsmusteranmeldung** → **2**

☐ **Abzweigung aus der Patentanmeldung (dem Patent)** →

_____ **P**

☐ Der Anmelder ist an **Lizenzvergabe** interessiert (unverbindlich)

(9) **Priorität** (inländische, ausländische, Ausstellungs-Priorität - Land, Prioritätstag u. Aktenz. d. Voranmeldung od. Ausstellung und Tag der erstmaligen Schaustellung)

(10) **Gebührenzahlung** in Höhe von _____ EUR

Erläuterungen
und Kosten-
hinweise s.
Rückseite

☐ **Einzugsermächtigung** Vordruck (A 9507) *ist beigefügt*

☐ **Überweisung** *(nach Erhalt der Empfangsbescheinigung)*

☐ Abbuchung von mehreren/unserem Abbuchungskonto bei der Dresdner Bank AG, München / Abbuchungsauftrag (A 124) ist beigefügt

Wird die Anmeldegebühr nicht innerhalb von 3 Monaten nach dem Eingang der Erklärung so gilt die Anmeldung als zurückgenommen!

(11) **Anlage**

1. _____ Seite(n) Beschreibung (2-fach)
2. _____ Seite(n) Schutzansprüche (2-fach)
   _____ Anzahl Schutzansprüche
3. _____ Blatt Zeichnungen (2-fach)
4. _____ Vertretervollmacht
5. _____ Abschrift(en) d. Voranmeldung(en) bei Priorität
6. _____ Abschrift der Voranmeldung bei Abzweigung

(12) Unterschrift(en)

G 6003
11.02

FOR GENERAL INFORMATION ONLY

30

The Application Form for the Utility Patent can be obtained from the Patent Office directly, say in writing. Much simpler and quicker however can it be downloaded from the Internet (www.dpma.de) and conveniently printed out at home. The correct form number reads: G 6003. Two file formats are offered: *doc* for Microsoft Word and *pdf* for the Adobe Reader.

If the form should have been downloaded as doc-format from the Patent Office server, then it is possible to fill it out and print it directly in Microsoft Word. The file was programmed in such a way that only permissible entries are possible and that the necessary copies are automatically filled out and printed.

One must pay attention to the fact that the submission of this Application Form alone, that is, without Description and/or without Claims is not sufficient to obtain an official date of registration. In order to obtain a valid confirmation of receipt and thereby a date of registration, you will need to submit the entire set of documents – that is, the *Application Form*, the *Description*, the *Claims* and, if necessary the *Drawings* - everything in double. The following fields you will find on the application form:

1. Postal Address: That postal address, to which the Patent Office is to send all letters concerning your application, and later concerning the patent. It can be either the address of the applicant, a delivery representative, or a representative like a lawyer. On the same height on the right side of the form is to be marked that this application concerns a Utility Patent application.

2. Emblem/Telephone/Date: An internal emblem can be indicated for reference in later correspondence. As date applies exclusively the confirmed entry date of the Patent Office for all future correspondence.

3. Function of the receiver: If at the receiver end it concerns a representative of the inventor, then the party to speak to should be submitted, except if the representative is a patent lawyer or an attorney.

4. Applicant/Representative: Use only if the address of the applicant and of the representative is not the same as the address of the indicated receiver.

5. Code number: Given by the Patent office

6. Title of the invention: The most precise technical title of the idea or the product. It should be brief and short, thus not: "Chlorophyll-producing, hydrocarbon-based bio device for the independent preparation of own copies" but: "Grass seed". The actual innovations are not to be put in the title.

7. Other requests: Request for suspension (voluntary): Delays the time of entry, and thereby of the protective effect, up to 15 months. The protective effect begins only after entry.
A request for Search (voluntary) initiates a payable search. It can also be requested by third parties, and at any later point in time. Important to note: There is no repayment of fees - for instance in case of denial, in case of canceling the request etc.

8. Explanations: a) Splitting/exclusion: Registrations here are only necessary if the current registration itself is based on another own, already existing Utility Patent registration.
b) Divergence: Registrations are only necessary if the current registration is based on another own, already existing patent application.
c) License awarding: Noncommittal indication about whether the applicant has an interest in the license awarding. If "Yes" is indicated, then the new patent will be made public in the

official patent sheet. This indication can be recalled at any time, and it does not commit to anything.

9. Priority: Specifications are necessary only if the current registration refers to another own, already existing utility patent or patent application. The precedence, regarding which registration has priority over another, is determined by the day of receipt in the Patent Office. In case of extended or foreign registrations, it is then possible under certain conditions to take into consideration the date of an own earlier registration, the priority.

10. Fees: Here the total of the application fees is to be entered. Without a search the total is only 40 Euros. Including a Search it is 290 Euro (40 + 250). As is noted on the form, fee codes are to be indicated for the correct allocation of your payments. The code number for the application fee is "321100", that for the search fee is "321200".

11. Appendices: Since applications can be submitted very differently depending upon idea and applicant, the specified number of attached appendices is registered here.

12. Signatures: The signature of the applicants or his/her representatives.

2. The Description

1) **DESCRIPTION** to the application for a Utility Patent with the title

Transportable combination lock for summer- and winter sports equipment

of Mister Stefan Mustermann dd. 30.06.2006:

Field: Theft protection, mechanical locks. Starting point among other things were complaints and doubts of skiers about the theft of their ski equipment during the stay in a ski hut, restaurant etc. Usually the ski equipment is placed unsecured and unguarded outside against the house wall. Thefts then occur for example when a culprit with old worthless skis approaches, buckles new expensive skis and disappears.

This lind of theft can be prevented with the herein described system with the present functional appellation *SkiSafe*. In addition, even say, bicycles and light mopeds can be secured against unauthorized removal by suitable molding with SkiSafe.

In the following pages one form of a prototype is described, which can be manufactured at very small expense due to its simple structure. By using other molding, material choice, sort and position of the locking mechanism and functional structure of the handles, many more applications are conceivable.

The enclosed Drawings serves for a better overview; it represents only one of many possible application variants. Therefore is to be explicitly referred to that claims are submitted for all conceivable combinations:

Two (approximately) congruent sheet metal punchings in form of a handle are connected on one side and revolvable against each other to a mechanically lockable unit (Clamp):

The internal contour of the handles is formed in such a way that in the closed condition (at least) one pair of skis, and, if necessary, additionally a pair of ski sticks, closely fit in. At the system is a lock (or the device for a lock, some holes), so that the handles can repeatedly be locked and opened.

After the skis were set upward, ideally with the sliding surfaces to each other, the SkiSafe is folded up and locked between toe and heel receptacle of the ski connections. Thus, putting on the "parked" skis is no longer possible and unauthorized removal is prevented.

In order to make the system smaller for carrying it, one of the two handles gets along its center line (neutral fiber) a slotted hole or a guide groove. At the other handle is a guide pin, suitable for the groove or the slotted hole, attached. Thus the handles can (approximately) be pushed congruently one above the other, whereby the size of the system is being reduced by approx. 50% - the unit can be carried more comfortably, for example in a clothing bag.

34

The Description serves the fast conception of the new idea, which has to be understood by persons, who so far don't know nothing about it. The text is to explain 1. completely, 2. unmistakably and 3. precisely the idea or invention.

There is no form for it. Apart from the deep understanding of the own idea a successful and complete description depends thus on a certain art of formulating. This requirement should not be under-estimated: If and when a patent controversy arises, and the so-called Claims do not allow a final desicion – then the Description (and if existing, the Drawings) might make the difference. The applicant formulates thus in his/her very own interest.

After one is familiar with the fundamental requirements for the written form (which are: A4 paper size, portrait orientation, etc., see above), then the text organization always follows the same rules:

- It always begins with the title. The title should correspond to the title mentioned in the Application Form.

- Then the indication of the technical area the invention belongs to follows, as well as a short description of the currently available technology. It then is described in short the lack of and/or possibilities for improvement.

- The following main part must make very clear by which means the inventor has solved this problem.

- The invention is then described in more detail by means of an real world application example. In this example further details are to be indicated.

- References to Drawings can be used for better understanding. However, the Description itself must not contain any drawings or sketches.

- The description is finalized with the attained advantages of the new item.

3. The Claims

2) **CLAIMS** to the application for a Utility Patent with the title

Transportable combination lock for summer- and winter sports equipment

of Mister Stefan Mustermann dd. 30.06.2006:

1) Transportable combination lock for summer- and winter sports equipment, identified by

two handles being connected in a fulcrum.

2) System according to claim 1, identified by

both handles being formed approximately congruently.

3) System according to claim 1 and 2, identified by

being structurally so arranged, that the handles can be glided approximately congruently either one above the other or into one another.

4) System according to claim 1, 2 and 3, identified by

being structurally so arranged, that the handles can be locked in the closed condition.

5) System according to claim 1, 2, 3 and 4, identified by

the handles being formed in such a way, that at least one pair of skis can fit in them.

6) System according to claim 1, 2, 3, 4 and 5, identified by

the handles being formed in such a way, that it is also possible to install them on two-wheeled motor vehicles for the purpose of the prevention of the unauthorized use.

7) System according to claim 1, 2, 3, 4, 5 and 6, identified by

the handles being formed in such a way that aside from the main function of "protection against theft", the system can fulfill one or more auxiliary functions, like for example "grippers" and/or "screwdriver" etc.

FOR GENERAL INFORMATION ONLY !

37

A comprehensive and complete formulation of the Claims is a – if not *the* – substantial core of each Utility Patent application. It is mainly it, neither the Description nor the Drawings, which determines the scope of protection and thus the value of the patent right.

It cannot be pointed out strongly enough that those technical characteristics, which are contained in the Claims, are the very basis for each and every later right on the invention. Therefor, it is very important to take extra-ordinarily care of their elaboration. If not already done, the delegation to a patent lawyer just for this subtask could easily prove to be a good and worthwhile descision.

In order to give the reader an idea of how important this point is: We hereby expressly point out that exclusively the reader and/or his/her representing lawyer is responsible for all formulations and processing of his/her utility patent request. This book and the examples herein serve only as noncommittal information. In no case whatsoever it can be assumed of completeness or correctness.

As is true also for the Description, no special form exists for the Claims. And likewise the same formal requirements (which are: A4 paper size, portrait orientation, etc., see above) apply here. Even the text layout follows again the same rules :

- One begins with the title. This should correspond with the title in the application request.

- Claims should not contain references to the Description or to Drawings.

- In the identifying part, those characteristics of the invention are to be registered for which protection is requested. The identifying part is to be introduced by words as "identified through", or "thereby identified that.." or corresponding idioms.

- It is helpful, if one answers oneself the following questions: Of which parts does the device consist? Where the parts are concretely fitted? How are which parts connected with one another? etc...

- The formal style and the arrangement of the terms of the Claims are important. This should be done clearly and with sequential numbers. Individual characteristics are to be clearly cleared from the text and should always begin in a new line.

4. The Drawings

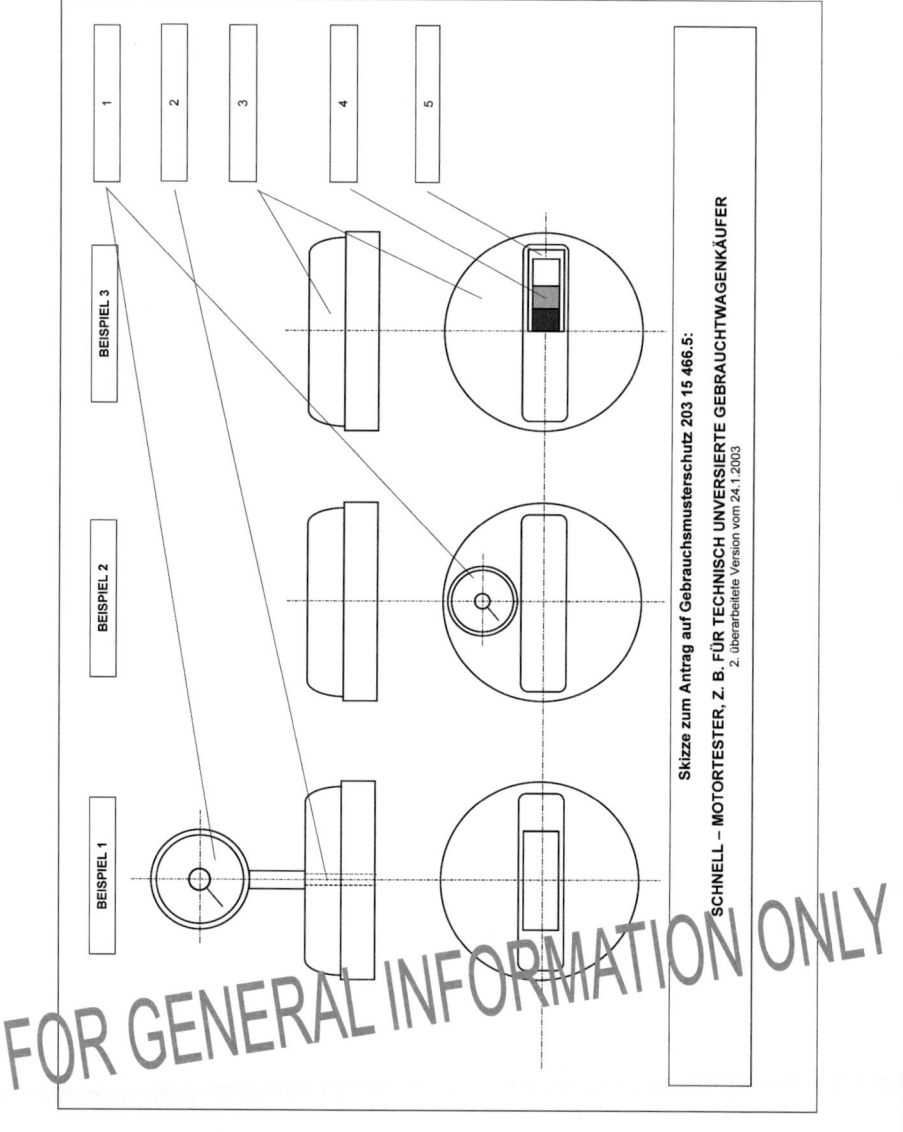

BEISPIEL 1   BEISPIEL 2   BEISPIEL 3

Skizze zum Antrag auf Gebrauchsmusterschutz 203 15 466.5:

SCHNELL – MOTORTESTER, Z. B. FÜR TECHNISCH UNVERSIERTE GEBRAUCHTWAGENKÄUFER

2. überarbeitete Version vom 24.1.2003

FOR GENERAL INFORMATION ONLY

40

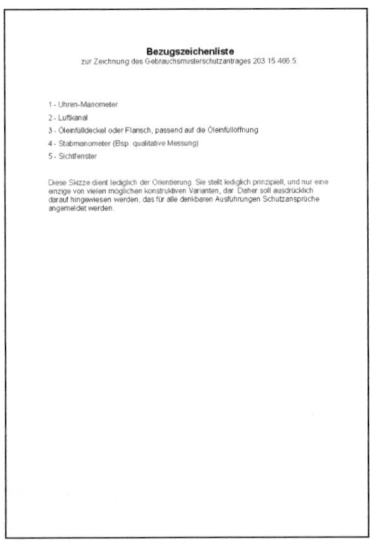

Drawings can serve the fast conception of a new idea and can prevent misunderstandings. They can unmistakably show the substantial characteristics of an invention with only a few lines. They should show all characteristics and their interaction clearly and emphasize the most important. Unimportant and insignificant details can be omitted. A drawing standard adequate to technical blue prints, like they are used in industry and trade, is not required. "Good sketches" describe the formal requirements of the Patent Office better. For example, often they can be drawn properly with the design elements of MS-Word. As well as for Description and Claims, for the Drawings there is no form provided. The same well-known form requirements (which are: A4 paper size etc.) apply (except for paper orientation):

- No obligation for a Drawing exists for an application for a Utility Patent. Nevertheless, often they are helpful.

- Drawings can be removed from the application if desired, as long as the application procedure is not yet finalized.

- Drawings *must* be submitted, if reference to them was made in the Claims or in the Description.

- Any kind of text, for example names or explanations, is not permitted in the Drawings! Individual parts are to be described by pure numbers only.

- If individual parts are provided with numbers for explanation, then a reference symbol list is to be provided.

- Photographs are not considered Drawings and cannot substitute these.

- Drawings must be submitted on separate sheets and in double.

5. After mailing

Often, you will receive your first mail from the Patent Office only a few days after the application was sent: The acknowledgement of receipt arrives. It concerns a copy of the application form for the applicant, which now carries a file reference number. In addition, the date of receipt has been punched into or printed onto the paper, by which this date officially is confirmed.

Now is the right time for paying: Transfer the application fee now. As long as the money is not received by the Patent Office, further processing of your application stays idle (the entry date, however, is still secured in your name) - until after three month it is deleted without notice, if one did not pay at all.

Only if you possess a lot of experience with applications of this kind, or if a patent lawyer worked for you, is it likely that nothing more happens until in a few weeks the Utility Patent certificate arrives by mail. In all other cases – according to noncommittal information by a patent office coworker – up to 80 % of all initial applications receive a deficiency notice with request for rectification of defects. In nearly all cases they object only against formulations or layouts.

To remedy deficiencies
A notice of deficiency from the Patent Office detailes the deficiencies and gives usually 4 weeks for the rectification of the defects. To make sure, and/or to avoid repeated back- and forth mailing, one can call the specialist in the Patent Office and discuss the intended improvements. Here it is important to know that the specialists of the Patent Office are in no way technical experts - but administrative and office procedure

specialists (according to my own experience nearly always friendly and helpful), who are trained on accurate adherence to the form requirements. They usually do not have any notion about technology:

1. **If a differently phrased formulation with the same meaning does not solve the problem,**

2. **..or if the requests for change, particularly within the Claims, go beyond your acceptance,**

3. **..or if the Claims would lose effectiveness,**

then you should <u>not</u> make <u>any</u> change, only because this is asked by the specialist! Rather ask for advice at a higher authority, for example a lawyer, or the opinion of the department head at the Patent Office.

With the mailing of the revision (for example: "1. revised version of the Claims of 11.10.2007 for utility patent application 203.555.1234 of 11. 10.2007") the case is usually settled.

All changes should be recorded and documented. Always keep copies with an exact date of all correspondence.

Registration and proclamation

If no formal deficiencies exist, or if the existing ones were eliminated and the registration fee has been paid, then your Utility Patent will be recorded in the Register of Utility Patents. The entry is published in the Patent Office Journal in Germany and you will receive a certificate by mail within a few weeks. Keep in mind 1. that your newly obtained rights may be worth quite something 2. that these rights are good only within the borders of Germany, but 3. that they can be extended to a full patent.

Addresses

The following list of German addresses concerning Utility Patents and regular patents was examined neither for completeness nor for quality. The entries serve exclusively the information and represent no recommendation. In each individual case the reader is solely responsible for his decisions. Any liability is excluded.

- Deutsches Patent- und Markenamt (DPMA), Zweibrückenstraße 12, 80331 München, Telefon (089) 21 95-0, Telefax (089)21 95-22 21, Telefonische Auskünfte (089)21 95-34 02, www.dpma.de, Postanschrift Deutsches Patent und Markenamt, 80297 München
- DPMA, Dienststelle Jena, Goethestraße 1, 07738 Jena, Telefon (03641) 40-54, Telefax. (03641) 40-56 90, Telefonische Auskünfte (03641) 40-55 55
- DPMA, Technisches Informationszentrum Berlin, 10958 Berlin, Telefon (030) 25 99 2-0, Telefax (030) 25 99 2-404, Telefonische Auskünfte (030) 25 99 2-22 0
- AGIT - Aachener Gesellschaft für Innovation und Technologietransfer mbH, Am Europaplatz, 52068 Aachen, Telefon (02 41) 9 63 - 10 20, Telefax (02 41) 9 63 - 10 33
- ATI Küste Agentur für Technologietransfer und Innovationsförderung GmbH, Joachim-Jungius-Straße 9, 18059 Rostock, Telefon (03 81) 4 05 93 11, Telefax (03 81) 4 05 93 10
- AXON Technologie Consult GmbH, Hanseatenhof 8, 28195 Bremen, Telefon (04 21) 1 75 55 – 15, Telefax (04 21) 17 16 86
- BTI - Beratungsgesellschaft für Technologietransfer und Innovationsförderung mbH, Gostritzer Straße 61-63, 01217 Dresden, Telefon (03 51) 8 71 75 61 / 75 55, Telefax (03 51) 8 71 75 56
- Bundesverband Deutscher Patentanwälte e.V., Kronenstraße 30, 70174 Stuttgart, Telefon (0711) 22 29 76-0, Telefax (0711) 22 29 76 –76, www.bundesverband-patentanwaelte.de
- Büro für Technologietransfer, Dipl.-Ing. Klaus Hübner, Schillerallee 15, 22926 Ahrensburg, Telefon (0 41 02) 58 482, Fax(0 41 02) 16 61
- COSEARCH COHAUSZ HASE Recherche GmbH, Schumannstraße 107, 40237 Düsseldorf, Telefon (02 11) 9 14 60 – 10, Telefax (02 11) 9 14 60 - 15
- Deutscher Erfinderring e.V. und Deutscher Erfinderverband e.V., Sandstr. 7, 90443 Nürnberg, Telefon (09 11) 26 98 11, Telefax (09 11) 26 97 80
- DVCG Deutsche Venture Capital Gesellschaft GmbH, Emil-von-Behring-Str. 2, D-60439 Frankfurt a. Main, Telefon (0 69) 5 70 06-0, Telefax(0 69) 5 70 06-200, www.dvcg.de

45

- Doitsugo Kaiwakyoshitsu Rita, Alexander Binner, 810-0001 Fukuoka-Shi, Chu-oku, Tenjin 6-6-3, Nagano Biru 2.F, Japan, Telefon/Telefax 0 92 (7 16) 62 12, E-Mail ritter@fat.coara.or.jp
- Edison & Co., Erfinderlokal mit der Möglichkeit, Ausstellungen, Erfinder-Stammtische, Vernissagen u.a. durchzuführen, Schulstraße 28, 80634 München, Telefon (0 89) 13 03 93 93, Telefax(0 89) 13 03 92 92
- Erfinderbüro Tiling, Dachshofstr. 12, 81249 München, Telefon (0 89) 85 66 39 37, Telefax(0 89) 85 66 39 38, www.erfinderbuero.de
- Erfinder-Kontaktstelle Hamburg, Buxtehuder Str. 76, 21073 Hamburg, Telefon (0 40) 35 90 58 46, Telefax (0 40) 35 90 58 58
- Erfinderzentrum Stubbe GmbH, Am Plessen 6, 49205 Hasbergen/Osnabrück, Telefon (0 54 05) 942 22, Telefax (0 54 05) 942 24
- EZN Erfinderzentrum Norddeutschland GmbH, Hindenburgstr. 27, 30175 Hannover, Telefon (05 11) 81 30 51, Telefax (05 11) 2 83 40 75
- Forschungsagentur Berlin GmbH, Köpenicker Straße 325, 12555 Berlin, Telefon (0 30) 6 57 29 64, Telefax (0 30) 65 76 23 51
- Forschungs- u. Entwicklungs-Zentrum - FEZ Witten GmbH, Alfred-Herrhausen-Straße 44, 58455 Witten, Telefon (0 23 02) 9 14 00 – 0, Telefax (0 23 02) 9 14 00 – 50
- Fraunhofer-Gesellschaft zur Förderung der angewandten Forschung e.V., Patentstelle für die Deutsche Forschung, Leonrodstraße 68, 80636 München, Telefon (0 89) 12 05 - 4 21, Telefax (0 89) 12 05 - 4 98
- Future Holding Aktiengesellschaft, Hermelin Str. 6-8, 33378 Rheda-Wiedenbrück, Telefon (0 52 42) 93 68 – 0, Telefax (0 52 42) 37 70 27
- The Generics Group, Harston Mill, Harston, Cambridge CB2 5NH, United Kingdom, Telefon +44 12 23 87 52 00, Telefax +44 12 23 87 52 01, www.generics.co.uk
- German Venture Partners®, Sartoriusstraße 38, 45134 Essen, Telefon (02 01) 4 35 16 – 0, Telefax (02 01) 4 35 16 – 18
- Gesellschaft zur Entwicklung und Vermarktung Innovativer Produkte mbH, Grefrather Straße 42, 47669 Wachtendonk-Wankum, Telefon (0 28 36) 91 49 – 0, Telefax (0 28 36) 91 49 – 99
- Glasauer Unternehmensbeteiligungen AG, Gelbinger Gasse 97, 74523 Schwäbisch Hall, Telefon (07 91) 97 33 88, Telefax (07 91) 97 33 89
- Global Inventions Ltd., Specialists In Marketing Patented Inventions H.K. Branch, Correspondence Address: Unit B, 9/F, Tung Wui Building, 46 Kimberley Road,Tsim Sha Tsui, Kowloon, Hong Kong, Telefon (00 852) 23 16 75 88
- Dr. Görlitz - Agency Technics, Achtern Höben 5, 21465 Wentorf b. Hamburg, Telefon (0 40) 7 20 49 49, Telefax (0 40) 7 20 38 26
- Handelskammer Hamburg IPC-Innovations- und Patent-Centrum, Adolphsplatz 1, 20457 Hamburg, Telefon (0 40) 3 61 38 - 4 44, Telefax (0 40) 36 13 82 70

46

- Heinz Krönauer, Werkstätte für Sondermaschinenbau, Marienthal 2, 94244 Geiersthal, Telefon (0 99 23) 80 22 55, Telefax (0 99 23) 80 22 57
- Ideenbörse GmbH, Badenerstr. 153, CH - 8003 Zürich, Telefon (00 41) 7 94 04 78 35
- IDEE PLUS, Am Krümmling 01, 06184 Dieskau, Telefon (03 45) 58 296 – 0, Telefax (03 45) 58 296 -40
- INSTI-Erfinderforum Bottwartal, Am Schloßberg 9, 71720 Oberstenfeld, Telefon (0 70 62) 2 18 84, Telefax (0 70 62) 2 18 11
- item communication management service GmbH, Dalbergstr. 18, 63739 Aschaffenburg, Telefon (0 60 21) 31 88 – 0, Telefax (0 60 21) 31 88 – 60
- Licentie Marketing Nederland B.V., Bogert 1 Eindhoven, P.O. Box 466, 5600 AL Eindhoven Netherlands, Telefon + (31 40) 2 65 36 81, Telefax + (31 40) 2 65 35 45
- LITCA - Licencing, Innovation & Technology Consultants Association e.V., (früher: Verband der Patentwirtschaftler), deutsche Ansprechstelle: Willi S. Heuft, Schatzberg 10, 88662 Überlingen, Telefon (0 75 51) 78 64, Telefax (0 75 51) 6 47 52
- LPS Group, Licensing Products and Services, Irene Schmitt, Dipl.-Ing., European Manager, 235, Southwark Bridge Road, London SW1 6LY, United Kingdom, Telefon +44 (0) 207 450 50 90, Fax +44 (0) 207 407 72 26
- Maria Fluske GmbH, Beschaffung von Risikokapital für Erfinder zur Anmeldung, von nationalen und internationalen Patenten, Heisbergstraße 6, 51570 Windeck, Telefon (0 22 95) 57 48, Telefax (0 22 95) 57 55
- MC Maragudakis Consulting, Am Schloßberg 9, 71720 Oberstenfeld, Telefon (0 70 62) 2 18 84, Telefax (0 70 62) 2 18 11
- MIPO - Mitteldeutsche Informations-Patent-Online-Service GmbH Halle, Rudolf-Ernst-Weise-Straße 18, 06112 Halle/Saale, Telefon (03 45) 29 39 80, Telefax (03 45) 2 93 98 40
- OPI OFFICE POUR LA PROMOTION L'INDUSTRIE GENEVOISE, François Brulhart, Rue Boissonnas 9, Case postale 1355, CH-1211 Genève 26, Telefon: +41 22-308 98 80, Telefax+41 22-308 98 90
- Patentanwaltskammer, Tal 29, 80331 München, Telefon (089) 24 22 78-0, Telefax (089) 24 22 78-24, www.patentanwalt.de
- Patentinformationszentrum der Hessischen Landes- und Hochschulbibliothek Darmstadt, Schöfferstraße 8, 64295 Darmstadt, Telefon (0 61 51) 16 - 55 27, Telefax (0 61 51) 16 - 55 28
- PAVIS e.G., Verrechnungs-, Informations- und Serviceorganisation der Patentanwälte in der Bundesrepublik Deutschland e.G., Prinzenweg 6a, 82319 Starnberg, Postfach 1546, 82305 Starnberg, Telefon (0 81 51) 76 50, Telefax: (0 81 51) 2 12 44
- Reburg-Patentverwertungsgesellschaft mit beschränkter Haftung, Wilhelm-Busch-Straße 2, D-38723 Seesen-Rhüden, Telefon (0 53 84) 9 65 41, Telefax (0 53 84) 96 54 45

Verlags Programm
Auszug

Erhältlich bei:

amazon.de

Libri.de

sowie im klassischen Buchhandel

Unsere Bestseller & Neuheiten

Allein gelassen? Die Exliebe wiedergewinnen

Wenn die Liebe zur Tür hinaus ist und alles nach lebenslangem Novemberwetter ausschaut, dann regiert die Sehnsucht pur: So schön wäre es, wieder von ihm/ihr in den Arm genommen zu werden. Dieser Ratgeber enthält eine ausführliche Schritt-für-Schritt Anleitung für Ihren möglichen Anfang vom Happy-End: Leicht verständlich sind mehrere Psychologieprinzipien zusammengefaßt, um Ihrer Ex-Liebe das „Ex" sanft aus der Hand zu nehmen. 4. Auflage 2010 · 12 x 19 cm · Euro 7,90 · ISBN 978-3-8311-1825-0. Auch in 2 erweiterten Ausgaben erhältlich (siehe nächste Seite).

Die Grundregeln des Erfolgs. So werden Sie erfolg-
reich. Ob in der Partnerschaft, im Beruf, oder beim Kontostand – erfolgreich werden Menschen überall auf der Welt auf ähnliche Weise, weil alle Menschen einer ähnlichen Psychologie folgen. In diesem Ratgeber erfahren Sie die Grundregeln jedes Erfolges. So können Sie ab sofort die richtigen Entscheidungen in Ihrem Leben treffen. Denn es ist Ihres, und Sie haben nur eines. Nur Sie allein bestimmen Ihre Ziele, und ob Sie diese Ziele erreichen. Oder ob Sie sich abbringen, ablenken oder bevormunden lassen. 2010 · 12 x 19 cm · Euro 9,95 · ISBN 978-3-8391-2049-1

Auswandern. Die wichtigsten Schritte

Wer hat nicht schon einmal daran gedacht: In einem anderen Land leben. Entweder regelmäßig für ein paar Monate, oder gleich ganz: Tropisches Meer oder alpine Berge genießen. Freier und freundlicher seine Tage verbringen, vielleicht sogar kostengün-stiger. Doch wie geht das überhaupt - auswandern ? In diesem Ratgeber werden die wichtigsten Schritte jeder Auswanderung beschrieben: Was sind die Grundvoraussetzungen ? Wie wird die Abreise und Ankunft geschickt vorbereitet ? Und was müssen die ersten Schritte im Wunschland sein ? 2010 · DIN A5 · Euro 8,95 · ISBN 978-3-8391-2273-0

Allein gelassen ? Die Exliebe wiedergewinnen ...
und zusammenbleiben!

Zusätzlich zur ausführlichen Schritt-für-Schritt Anleitung aus dem bekannten Titel „Allein gelassen ? Die Exliebe wiedergewinnen" enthält dieser Ratgeber genaue Erläuterungen, wie aus Ihrer wiederhergestellten Beziehung eine dauernde Partnerschaft wird: Mehr als 25 konkrete Einzelratschläge zum täglichen Zusammensein unterstützen Sie, ein langes und glückliches Leben zu zweit aufzubauen. 2. Auflage 2009 · 12 x 19 cm · Euro 11,90 · ISBN 978-3-8330-0692-0. Kurzausgabe: **Allein gelassen? Die Exliebe wiedergewinnen...und die 10 wichtigsten Tips zum Zusammenbleiben!** 2008 · Euro 9,90 · ISBN 978-3-8370-6876-4

Deutscher Patentschutz für 40 Euro
Wie Ihre kleinen Ideen & Erfindungen großes Geld verdienen

Irgendwann hat jeder eine gute Produktidee. Doch Gelderfolg stellt sich selten ein, weil wertvolles geistiges Eigentum ungeschützt bleibt: „...Zu kompliziert, zu teuer.." lautet meist die Begründung. Dabei ist echter deutscher Patentschutz bereits für 40 Euro erhältlich: Bis zu 10 Jahre lang, und ohne Anwaltszwang. Hier wird das offizielle Patentamts-Verfahren samt dem einfachen Antrag leichtverständlich vorgestellt. 2. akt. Auflage 2009 · DIN A5 · Euro 7,95 · ISBN 978-3-8334-2638-4. Auch in englischer Sprache erhältlich.

Ein gebrauchtes Auto kaufen
Die wichtigsten Tips & Tricks für Nicht-Techniker

Auf dem Privatmarkt gibt es häufig bessere und günstigere Angebote als beim Händler – wenn man sich nur ein wenig auskennt. Aber wie finden sich die guten Angebote unter den zahlreichen fragwürdigen? Hier erfahren die Leser wichtige Tips & Tricks vom Diplom-Ingenieur und können viel Geld sparen: 1. Welche Anzeigen Sie besser nicht anrufen. 2. Wie Sie geschickt mit dem Verkäufer umgehen. 3. Wie Sie versteckte Mängel entdecken. 2007 · DIN A5 · Euro 7,95 · ISBN 978-3-8334-9079-8

Frauen zum Heiraten verführen

Heiraten – das höchste Ziel einer guten Partnerschaft auf ihrem Weg zur besten. Doch wenn „die Beste von allen" noch nicht so recht überzeugt ist, dann hilft dieser Ratgeber dem modernen Mann: Für zahlreiche Alltagssituationen erfährt der Leser leicht verständliches und einfach anzuwendendes, psychologisches Know-How, um in ihrem Kopf die Hochzeitsgedanken hüpfen zu lassen: So schön kann Zweisamkeit werden. 2010 · 12 x 19 cm · Euro 8,90 · ISBN 978-3-8391-1885-6

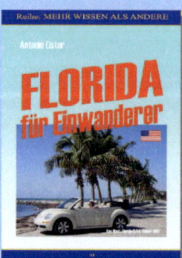

Florida für Einwanderer

Sonne, Palmen und Meer – damit ist für die meisten Menschen Florida, der tropische Bundesstaat der USA, beschrieben. Doch wer hier länger leben möchte als 2 Wochen, wer vielleicht gar Resident sein möchte, dem nutzt das typische Urlaubswissen nur wenig. In diesem Ratgeber wird Florida für Einwanderer beschrieben: Seine Geographie, das Klima, die Wirtschaft und Politik. Danach erfahren Sie alles Nötige über das Wohnen, Arbeiten, die Steuern und vieles mehr aus erster Hand. 2009 · DIN A5 · Euro 9,95 · ISBN 978-3-8370-8866-3

Dick sein – Nein Danke!

Schlank werden und sein – für viele moderne Menschen ein Dauerthema. Dabei ist Abnehmen viel einfacher als die Meisten glauben: Jeder Körper kann auf ein frei gewähltes Wunschgewicht „eingestellt" werden. Leichtverständliche Kenntnisse reichen aus, denn die mächtige MMF-Regel macht es möglich: Schöner, gesünder und sogar kostengünstiger leben, kurz: Endlich glücklich sein. Hier erfahren Sie das Grundgesetz jedes Schlankseins – ohne Kosten zum Sofortstart geeignet. 2010 · 12 x 19 cm · Euro 8,95 · ISBN 978-3-8391-0921-2

Wegziehen in die USA
Das Wichtigste zu Visa, Wohnung, Arbeit, Auto, Finanzen

Die USA sind Top-Einwanderungsziel unserer Erde. Dieser Ratgeber ist die Basis für den ersten Schritt in das Land der unbegrenzten Möglichkeiten. Konkret wird der Leser über die wichtigsten Fragen informiert: Visaarten, Kauf und Miete von Wohnung und Haus, Stellensuche, Selbstständigkeit, Autokauf und Finanzen werden zu einem günstigen Preis nahegebracht. 2002 · DIN A5 · Euro 6,95 · ISBN 978-3-8311-4048-0.

Der richtige Lizenzvertrag für Patent-Inhaber und Erfinder

In „Deutscher Patentschutz für 40 Euro" wird gezeigt, wie das eigene geistige Eigentum zügig und kostengünstig beim Deutschen Patentamt geschützt wird. Doch wie erhält man dann einen Lizenzvertrag ? Und was gehört hinein ? Hier wird ein echter Vertrag zwischen Erfinder und Produktionsunternehmen Punkt für Punkt vorgestellt und erläutert. So erhalten Sie wertvolle Unterstützung, um bares Geld zu sparen und zu verdienen: Bei Lizenzgebühren, Anwaltsauslagen und durch Erinnerung an Vertragsrisiken, an die nicht jeder denkt. 2009 · DIN A5 · Euro 9,95 · ISBN 978-3-8370-8867-0

Männer zum Heiraten verführen. 40 Do's & Don'ts

Heiraten – für viele Frauen das romantischste Ziel einer guten Partnerschaft auf ihrem Weg zur besten. Doch falls „der Beste von allen" noch nicht so recht überzeugt ist, oder die Beziehung noch etwas Feinschliff benötigt, dann hilft dieser Ratgeber der modernen Frau. In 40 Einzelpunkten erfährt die Leserin leicht verständliches und einfach anzuwendendes psychologisches Wissen, um in seinem Kopf die Hochzeitsgedanken hüpfen zu lassen. 2003 · 12 x 19 cm · Euro 8,90 · ISBN 978-3-8311-4235-4

Auswandern. Die menschliche Seite.

Hier wird die menschliche, die emotionelle Seite einer Auswanderung geschildert: Warum und wieso eigentlich weg aus Deutschland? Wie steht der Partner dazu? Und was wird aus der Beziehung in der Ferne? Die wahren Erlebnisse eines jungen Paares aus Deutschland – erst ins entfernte Neuseeland, dann in die USA – faszinieren und machen gleichzeitig nachdenklich: Innig liebend zu zweit, plötzlich allein und verlassen, dann zwei neue »Love Birds« in einem neuen, traumhaften Leben: Wer nicht aufgibt, der erreicht seine Ziele. 2010 · 12 x 19 cm · Euro 9,95 · ISBN 978-3-8370-9291-2

Wohnsitz Florida – so klappts!

Um sich in den USA erfolgreich niederzulassen, sei es zeitweilig oder permanent, ist viel amerikanisches Know-how notwendig. Die Wohnsitz-Ratgeber über Florida und Kalifornien sind umfassende, detaillierte Handbücher zu dem jeweiligen US-Bundesstaat: Visamöglichkeiten, Hauskauf, Autokauf, Steuern, Stellensuche - kurz, das komplette Gewusst-Wie zum Leben genießen in den USA erfährt der Leser aus erster Hand. Ebenso enthalten sind viele ausgewählte Tips, Anschriften und Internetadressen, wie sie nur die Praxis liefern kann. **Florida:** 2000 · DIN A5 · Euro 15,29 · ISBN 978-3-89811-216-1 **Kalifornien:** 2000 · DIN A5 · Euro 15,29 · ISBN 978-3-8981-1332-8

100 verblüffende Autogeheimnisse

Nur wenige Menschen ahnen, welche verblüffenden Geheimnisse die erfolgreichste Maschine der Erde verbirgt. In diesem Buch wird erstaunliches Auto-Wissen leicht verständlich vorgestellt. Wer sich nicht sicher ist, wieviel PS ein Pferd hat, wie ein Kühler in 5 Minuten selbst repariert wird, ob die „James-Bond-Wende" wirklich funktioniert, daß Autos viel grüner sind als ICE-Züge...und weitere 96 Tatsachen wissen möchte, die üblicherweise Kfz-Ingenieuren vorbehalten bleiben – der erfährt hier weithin unbekannte Eigenschaften unserer Autos. 2002 · DIN A5 · Euro 15,90 · ISBN 978-3-8311-1826-7

▶ **Tips & Tricks zu GreenCard und B-Visa** Die USA sind Top-Einwanderungsziel unserer Erde. Dieser Ratgeber informiert alle Menschen, die sich zeitweise oder permanent dort niederlassen möchten über die beiden gängigsten Visaformen. Er erklärt die Unterschiede zwischen GreenCard und B1/B2 Visum, und worauf es bei den amerikanischen Behörden bei der Beantragung ankommt. 2000 · DIN A5 · Euro 6,60 · ISBN 978-3-89811-159-1

▶ **Bevor es zu spät ist. Die Trennung verhindern** Wenn zu spüren ist, daß die Liebe zur Tür hinaus will, dann ist es höchste Zeit zu reagieren. Doch wie können Sie Ihre Beziehung noch retten ? Hier erfahren Sie mehr als 30 wertvolle Tips aus der praktischen Psychologie, damit Ihr Partner seine Trennungsgedanken noch einmal überdenkt. Bevor es zu spät ist, können Sie mithilfe dieses Ratgebers einen fundierten Rettungsversuch für Ihre Beziehung unternehmen. Gleichzeitig legen Sie die Grundsteine für eine lange und glückliche Beziehung – gerade jetzt, wenn es so gar nicht danach ausschaut. 2009 · 12 x 19 cm · Euro 8,95 · ISBN 978-3-8370-8865-6

▶ **Alltag graut – Yachtbesitz bräunt** „Durchschnitts-Landratte wird Schiffsbesitzer" - wer hat davon noch nicht geträumt? Hier ist der Beweis, daß wirklich jeder Mann und jede Frau ein neues Leben beginnen kann. Spannend und unterhaltsam werden die Erlebnisse eines völlig boots-unerfahrenen Menschen aus Deutschland erzählt – auf seinem Weg zum süßen, unbeschwerten Leben auf der eigenen Yacht in Florida: Ab sofort ist jedes Jahr das beste Jahr. 2000 · 12 x 19 cm · Euro 12,74 · ISBN 978-3-8981-1334-2

▶ **Amerika: Visa•Wohnen•Arbeiten•Auto•Finanzen** Aufbauend auf „Wegziehen in die USA" liefert dieser Ratgeber noch detailliertere USA-Informationen, die weit über das übliche Urlaubswissen hinausgehen: Visaformen, Hauskauf und Anmietung, Stellensuche, Firmengründung, Autokauf, Führerscheine, Banken und Steuern. 2001 · DIN A4 · Euro 9,95 · ISBN 978-3-8311-1922-6

▶ **Tipps & Tricks für Autofahrer** Praktisches Auto Know-How spart Geld im Alltag, hilft weiter und macht Spaß – besonders, wenn es sogar manchem Automechaniker unbekannt ist: Hier werden verblüffende Tips & Tricks rund um das Auto vorgestellt, die jeder Mann und jede Frau anwenden kann. So wird das Konto bei Reparaturen und beim Gebrauchtwagenkauf geschont, und der Leser weist sich bei Freunden und Bekannten als gewiefter Fachmann aus. 2004 · DIN A5 · Euro 5,95 · ISBN 978-3-8334-0764-2

▶ **Hexen heute erkennen** Viele Menschen wissen intuitiv: In unserer Welt existieren Kenntnisse und Fähigkeiten, die den Wissenschaften verborgen bleiben, und von denen nur wenige zu träumen wagen: Wirkliche Hexen sind unter uns. Daß die klugen Zauberinnen, zu unrecht oft als „böse" abgestempelt, heutzutage nicht als alte Frauen mit schwarzer Katze auftreten, ist vielen klar. Doch wie sind sie dann auszumachen? Und sollte man das überhaupt versuchen? 2005 · 12 x 19 cm · Euro 8,90 · ISBN 978-3-8334-3192-0

▶ **Land in Feindeshand – Deutschland wird sozialistisch** Viele Anzeichen der deutschen und europäischen Politik geben Anlaß zu Sorge: Um die persönliche Freiheit, um persönliches Eigentum und um die kommende Generation. Zeichen totalitärer Prinzipien und Denkweisen verstärken sich. Zieht schon wieder der häßliche und latent kriminelle Sozialismus auf? 2003 · 12 x 19 cm · Euro 9,90 · ISBN 978-3-8330-0485-8

▶ **Tanken für 0,99 (DM)** Für alle Dieselfahrer und an Technik interessierte Menschen: Dieselmotoren sind Mehrstoffmaschinen, die mit verschiedenen Kraftstoffen zuverlässig arbeiten. Wie und wo das eigene Diesel-Fahrzeug mit VEGA 9010, dem günstigen, überall erhältlichen und umweltfreundlichen Spar-Kraftstoff betankt wird, das beschreibt dieser Ratgeber. Ohne Umbaukosten! 2001 · 12 x 19 cm · Euro 9,95 · ISBN 978-3-8311-2173-1